Construction
Purchasing Success Guide

Stay on Budget through your Supply Chain Management

David Pollock

CONTENTS

Introduction

I want to thank you and congratulate you for purchasing the book, "Construction: Purchasing Success Guide, Stay on Budget through your Supply Chain Management"

This book contains proven steps and strategies on how to choose the right supplier, increase your profits, be efficient in your procurement and supply chain management and many more!

Whether you are a Small Business Owner, a Purchasing Agent/Manager for a large company, CEO or in any occupation where you rely on partnering with people to accomplish your profit, customer service, or personal goals, then this book is for you.

Thanks again for purchasing this book. I hope you enjoy it!

Chapter 1

Understanding Supply Chain Management

In construction, like in many other type of business, supply chain management tends to be taken for granted. Regardless of the business or the industry, it is important to realize that the supply chain is the glue that holds the whole business together. It starts with the procurement of the services or the materials that are needed to produce the end product. From there, it goes on, continuing through a line, until the customer has the finished product in his or her possession. In the construction industry, that would a finished building or structure of some description. The entire process involves a high level of decision-making and a number of "transaction" between the parties involved.

The Supply Chain

In order for the supply chain to work and to be cost effective, there are a number of trails that must be followed. First, the vendor/s have to be decided on for the purchase of the materials and/or services. Freight carriers must be chosen, if needed and solutions for warehousing. Storage and handling of the inventory has to be managed, and the marketing and distribution finalizes the chain.

In essence, supply chain management is all about decisions. Every single decision about the entire construction project, from breaking ground right through to handing over the structure to the customer must be included. The best way to truly understand the supply chain management is to understand the three levels of decision making that go into it.

Strategic Planning

The very first part to effective supply chain management is strategy and that start with making the most solid long-term decisions that will benefit the entire project and the parties involved. At this level, the groundwork is laid for the entire process and it is the most essential part of the management. Without making the decisions at this stage, you cannot possible develop a strategy or process for the rest of the project.

The issues that are dealt with at this stage include:

- Choosing the site for the project
- Determining the purpose of any business facilities required
- Creating a solid network of reliable transporters, suppliers and logistics handles
- Determining long-term improvements and innovative ideas that will meet the demands of the client
- Determining the management of the inventory and the product from beginning to end
- Deciding which IT systems and programs are needed for effective and efficient project handling

Product Development

The senior managers of the company have to define the direction the project will take when considering the kind of product they manufacture. In the case of construction, they will be working to either a specific blueprint, a developer, or another kind of client. In terms of general supply chain management, decisions have to be made on whether to develop an existing product or introduce a new one, or whether the current one can be rationalized.

The decisions may include deciding whether another company should be acquired or whether to sell of parts of their own existing company but, whatever the decisions are, the overall objective of the company should be the deciding factor.

Customers

At the strategic level, management must identify the customers to target for its current product or service. In construction, most companies are tendering for a new project or are building for an existing customer or developer. At this stage, advertising and marketing is also determined.

Manufacturing

Management must make decision on the infrastructure and the technology needed for the manufacturing process or, in this case, the construction process. Their decisions are made based on forecasts and estimates and will take into account the materials they use and how they are manufactured. Decisions must be made on the way in which the product is constructed and this may include the requirement for new facilities to be built to handle the project. At this level, decisions must be made on whether to use third party logistics or subcontractors and they must also take into account any environmental issues surrounding the project.

Suppliers

Company management also has to decide which suppliers are going to be used for materials. One important consideration is the need to be able to reduce the amount spent on purchasing and increase profit, without compromising the safety, aesthetics or any other factor of the project. The suppliers must be chosen carefully and that may mean using global suppliers instead of local ones, to gain greater discounts, providing quality is maintained.

Logistics

Logistics is a very important part of supply chain management. Decisions need to be made on the logistics network; in construction, many companies use their own people to pick up and deliver the materials needed and that means decisions must be made on warehousing, mode of transportation and, in some cases, it may be determined that it is more cost effective to use third party subcontractors to do the work.

Strategic decision-making is what determines the entire project and the direction it takes. These decisions should be made taking the company objectives into account and they can be refined as and when the needs of the company change and they also allow for the operational and tactical decisions to be made.

Tactical Management

All businesses, regardless of the industry, must make short-term decisions that involve the entire supply chain on a tactical basis. In the strategic planning level, the decisions are made and the plans are laid for the project. However, when it comes to defining the actual processes used, that comes down to tactical level. The decisions made at this level will determine how risks are kept to a minimum and how costs are controlled. The focus is now on the needs and demands of the customer and how to achieve the best value.

The common decisions made at tactical levels are:

- Choosing and procuring the contracts needed for the services and materials required
- Settlement of the production schedules and the safety guidelines, as well as guidelines for quality and quantity
- Solutions for warehousing and transportation, including any third parties or other subcontractors needed
- Management of inventory, including the storage and distribution if needed

- Comparing competitors and laying out the best practice guide

The tactical level is where the measures are adopted to save money for the company and the decisions are made according to the strategic level decisions made by management. While the strategic planning covers the entire supply chain, tactical level focuses on how to create the real benefits for the company, in the following areas.

Manufacturers

Company management will decide on how many manufacturing sites are needed and where they will be. However, when it comes to determining the cost of production that comes down to tactical management. Where applicable, decisions have to be made on methods of manufacture, technologies used and how to do it all at the best cost without compromising the integrity of the company or the project.

Logistics

While strategic planning looks at the function of in-house logistics, tactical management may take the decision to outsource the logistics to save money. The same goes for warehousing needs – tactical manages may determine that it is cheaper to lease warehouse facilities than it is to build.

Suppliers

Global suppliers can often offer better benefits in terms of cost than local ones and tactical management has to come up with the best plan for terms and savings based on the decisions made at strategic level.

Product Development

If a company is committed to producing a specific line of products, they have to make tactical decisions on which ones are developed, the specifications of the product, the distribution area and the market where the most profit can be gained.

Tactical decision is made based on the strategic level plan, which is based on the objectives of the company. Once tactical decisions have been made, it comes down to operational level.

Operational Level

This is, or should be, the most obvious part of the supply chain management. This level is where the decisions are made on daily processes and the planning required to keep the supply chain working as it should be. One of the biggest mistakes that man companies make is to focus on operational level without considering the strategic and tactical levels. To be effective, the operational level must be based within the framework built by the previous two processes. Some of the aspects that are considered are:

- Forecasting supply and demand on a daily and weekly basis
- Production including details of the management of goods-in-process and scheduling
- Monitoring logistics to ensure that contracts and orders are fulfilled
- Settling loss and damage claims with clients, suppliers and vendors
- Management of the materials that are moving in and out as well current inventory

Decisions made at this level are made to make sure that the supply chain moves effectively and efficiently with the maximum benefit in terms of cost.

Manufacturing

The tactical decisions lay out the terms of manufacturing. However, at operational level, they have to deal with problems that arise from manufacturers not being able to rely on suppliers. Decisions must be made about keeping certain things in stock to make sure that the production line can continue. Although this may raise the costs, if the production line stopped because of a lack of stock, the costs incurred would be even higher.

Suppliers

The decisions on using global suppliers and negotiation for contracts are done strategic level. While this can offer up considerable savings in costs, local sites may need to make decisions at operational level with their suppliers to make sure the supply chain is running efficiently. It may be that negotiations must be carried out regarding quality, especially if the global supplier is from a country where the quality standards are not so high – operations managers may need to negotiate that the supplier come up with a higher quality product to ensure quality throughout the entire project.

Logistics

Much of the focus in the strategic and tactical levels may be on the use of third party logistics, mainly because it can represent a substantial savings to the company and, in many cases, these third party companies are integrated into the supply chain. However, if a particular company cannot make a delivery in a certain area, decisions must be made at operational level on whether to lease a local warehouse or to negotiate with other logistics companies.

As you can see, every part of the supply chain has its own role to play and all parts must work with the others. Strategic and tactical management decisions are made to try to save the company money while maintaining quality and efficiency. At operational level, many decisions have to be made on a daily basis and must be made within the framework laid down by the strategic and tactical managers. If one part fails, the whole supply chain fails.

Chapter 2

Supply Chain Management in Construction

The last chapter looked at the concepts of supply chain management overall, now it's time to look at the construction industry. The original concept of SCM came from JIT (Just-in-Time) logistics and production and it has flourished in the manufacturing industry. Today, supply chain management is seen as an autonomous concept at managerial level, although it is still mostly dominated by the logistics side of business.

Supply chain management offers up a methodical way to deal with control, identifying where wastage occurs, among other problems, caused by myopic control. The construction industry supply chain is plagued with these kinds of problems.

A typical supply chain for a construction project would most likely include engineers, architects, prime contractors, subcontractors, and suppliers, all of whom come together to build the requirements of an owner or developer. It is a complicated supply chain that is characterized by short-term relationships that are often adversarial, all driven by the competitive process of bidding for the job.

Management of the construction supply chain tends to focus on lean construction strategies, including:

- JIT purchasing
- Evaluation of suppliers

- Selection of subcontractors
- Management of the relationship with subcontractors
- Acquisition of equipment
- Sharing information
- Quality control

Who is and isn't included in the supply chain

Right now, many companies still work in a one-dimensional view, a view in which the
only relationships considered are those on the surface level. In order to understand and appreciate the variety of requirements and interests down the supply chain, a three-dimensional view is needed. If a specific party adds value to the project, they should be included in the supply chain but this must be looked at a long-term view instead of the short-term attitude in place today.

Historically, too many important parties have been looked out of the supply chain management process, for whatever reason. It is important, if the supply chain is to work to the benefit of the company, that every single party is involved at some point during the process. However, including everybody right from the start can complicate matters so careful consideration has to be given to who is included from the start and who is brought in at a later date, as and when needed. The construction supply chain is actually two chains – a main one and a contributory chain and these are used to include the right people at the right time.

Removing Waste and Improving the Supply Chain

As I said earlier, many construction supply chains involve a lot of waste and can be substantially improved to make savings. Some of the key issues that have to be determined are:

Decisions must not be made on a "price" bass; they should be made on a "cost" basis

Modularization of materials should be done where possible to standardize the entre chain and to simplify matters

All activity must be evaluated and then improved on or simplified where possible

Although things have improved significantly in recent times, the construction industry is known for not using best practice or for learning from mistakes made in other sectors. It is important for changes to be identified and applied where needed, taking note of the processes in other sectors.

How to Improve Construction Supply Chain Performance

In order for improvement to be made, all of the individual parties involved in the chain must come together to identify the problem areas and push the changes through where needed. This should be done through:

- Education
- Cultural changes
- The understanding that the improvements will benefit everyone
- An open approach, shared by all, to the benefits of the improvements
- The right attitude and approach to participation in the supply chain
- Pre-planning
- Complete visibility

The management of subcontractors is an important part of the supply chain and a more effective way of managing includes:

- Regarding the subcontractor as a valued member of the supply chain

- Sharing the entire project picture with them
- Sharing the supply chain value with them
- Asking them for their input

Supply chain management is a huge part of the construction industry and must be implemented if cost savings are to be made and the project remains on-budget or under-budget throughout the whole chain.

In the next chapter, we look at how to manage the financial supply chain.

Chapter 3

Managing the Financial Supply Chain

While most companies, no matter what industry they are in, devote a great deal of time to the management of the physical supply chain, many tend to neglect the financial chain and it is this side that needs the most attention. Costs are escalating and it is vital that cash flow and capital are managed with the same, if not higher, level of attention that the physical supply chain is given. At the end of the day, if the financial side breaks down, the rest will follow because both chains are integrated to such an extent that each relies on the other.

Just so you know what we are talking about here, the financial chain is the transactions that take place between the partners that purchase goods and service and those who pay for them, for example, sending out purchase orders or invoices and making the payments associated with them. Finance is so much more than "bean counting" and the financial supply chain is a representation of the lifeblood that keeps an organization alive. This is where the cash flow comes from to make sure that the company can continue to trade and employ people to ensure that they can carry on. Research shows that there are two main pressures that motivate a company to focus on their financial chain – the impact of demand volatility on cash flow and a risk of default by a trading partner. A volatility in demand adds internal pressure, in that a company needs to have more inventory in stock, and external pressures, in that, at certain times, demand will slow and that means cash coming in will slow. A trading partner default will have a serious impact on accounts receivable, with the need for an increase in the allowance for "doubtful" accounts.

Staying on the Same Page

As a case study, we will look at Toyota Industrial Equipment Manufacturing Inc. (TIEM). While this is not a construction company, it will demonstrate the need for the proper management of the financial supply chain.

At TIEM, it all starts with the process of budgeting, a process that allocates the right amount of money to the right places; this ensures that each department can fund its own operations. As soon as the budget has been developed and set, it is down to key members of the personnel to ensure that the budget targets are met, so that the financial performance of the company is sound. If the targets cannot be met, it is important that the capital expenditure plan is reviewed as soon as possible, to delay disbursements of cash to non-essential areas. This is so that the manufacturing can continue at a high level.

The finance department has to work hand in hand with the supply chain departments that cover all aspects of the business. It's up to the financial department to give each of the other department's regular reports to enable to them to make the right decisions on a daily basis, as well as being able to plan their budgets and capital expenditure. The vice presidents of each department are the key decision makers, together with the presidents and these are the people who drive the success of TIEM, for both short and long-term goals and targets. Their success in managing their financial supply chain comes down to communication and the fact that they meet every day to discuss what has happened and plan for the next day. Managers who are responsible for reporting to the executives also attend the meetings, ensuring that everyone who has a part to play is involved in the process of identifying issues and coming up with ways to deal with them.

Commodity Risk Management

As time goes by, more and more companies are turning global, looking for their materials to come from just about anywhere in the world. However, this also brings with it a high likelihood of commodity risk. Commodity process are highly volatile, as PepsiCo, the huge food and drinks manufacturer has discovered, to the point where experts cannot even predict the prices for the future any longer. Commodity risk management (CRM) is a huge part of the financial supply chain and, as such, needs to be monitored carefully if uncertainty is to be reduced while productivity remains on the increase.

PepsiCo manage their CRM process by way of a global center of excellence. There, the key decision makers from the financial side (accounts and treasury) are teamed up with the global procurement decision makers on the supply chain side. Their job is to develop standards, processed and standardize the performance tracking of global commodities across all the countries in which the company has a presence. It is vital that, in order to be able to better hedge commodity prices, the manufacturing side of the business is fully understood. To that end, the treasury department at PepsiCo works together with the manufacturing department to make sure that everyone is working on the same page. If there is any change made to the production cycle or any other issues that arise, they can have a significant impact on the strategy for commodities so communication is a vital point to ensure effete management through the entire financial supply chain.

Change to Traditional Roles

Accenture consulting firm has come up with an idea for companies to think about, in terms of the financial supply chain. They say that the whole process should begin with an integrated team, one that works for the physical supply chain and the financial supply chain. The team should be well versed in advanced operations, risk management, real options and in the techniques and tools needed for financial optimization. The goal of this idea is a complete transformation from the standard view, in which the focus is on real flows and facilities, to a view that focuses on financial performance, corporate risk and the risks and returns for shareholders.

Let's take Boeing Co, the aerospace manufacturers. They use multiple financial techniques in their product development decisions and in their strategic planning decisions. Some of those tools include:

- Demand modeling – price and quantity
- Risk and investment modeling
- Portfolio analysis
- Spreadsheet modeling

We all know Boeing as the company who designs and engineers the aircraft we fly in but what we don't know is how they include financial designs into their decisions. An example of this is, can they bring the cost of their units down by spending more money on automating some of the production process. Manufacturers need to evolve to where financial supply chains converge with physical supply chains and that means that traditional roles will have to change. The same applies to construction companies who need to keep their supply chain on or under budget to increase their profits.

Chapter 4

Why Is Logistics So Vital for Supply Chain Management?

Before we can answer that question, we should take a quick look at what logistics actually is. It is a vital part of supply chain management because it covers the planning and management of goods, information and services from the start to the finish of the entire project. Logistics is the part of the business that deals with traffic and transportation of goods and services, the shipping, the receiving, any import or export operations, warehouse, management of inventory, purchase, planning for the production cycle and the customer service side. It is a critical part of the supply chain because it is the only way to monitor the movement of the product and how cost effective the process is.

Improving Efficiency and Cutting Costs

As soon as the word economy sifted into the 21st century, logistics took off and, in less than 20 years, it has become a major influencer of the business of moving products in line with customer requirements. Companies began to see how costs could be reduced and productivity could be increased by using a system to manage logistics and to manage the entire company to raise performance levels.

Logistics involves creating relationships with warehouses,

shipping companies and suppliers and being able to connect all of these systems together through one automated system. This created a reduction in overheads, with faster delivery to customer, thus increasing the profits. Logistics come into the strategic planning level of the supply chain management system – at this point, it must be determined exactly what is needed, how to get the materials at the right price and speeding up the delivery of the product or services to the customer.

The simplification of the communication systems between each of the departments involved has helped to create a blueprint that reduces the overall costs by improving the understanding of what the company needs and visibility. The cost savings are made through reductions in warehouse costs and on purchasing that is based on supply forecasts as well as better management of inventory, better shipping and faster deliveries.

Transportation and Warehousing

Today, we are all connected to one another through the internet and social media and this has resulted in a rise on the expectations of the customer for getting products delivered faster. For a company to embrace this way of thinking, they must look at the physical location of the warehouses and the best use of software to handle purchase requests within seconds rather than the old way of dealing in days.

These days, the basis of all growth in any business is customer satisfaction; without it, the profits will not be there. So, it is down to each individual company to come up with the best logistics plan they can – the best deal in warehousing, transportation and deliveries to trade-off against performance to bring costs down. These are all integral parts of the supply chain process and without a good solid logistics plan, the rest will fall apart.

Although this section overs logistics planning in general the core components can be applied to construction companies. Instead of planning for customer deliveries and shipping, their logistic might cover the transportation of materials and storage of stock.

Chapter 5

"The Purchaser"

"Man VS Woman Buyer: A male buyer will pay $2 for a $1 item he needs, while a female will pay $1 for a $2 item she doesn't need, but is on sale!"

All joking aside, to be great in any area of business it's important to know the expected outcome and goals of that role. The area of product procurement is no different and having the right people in the right positions will go a long way to its success and profitability. It is of great significance to reevaluate what goes on in a supply chain. The beauty in knowing the basics of supply chain management, is that we get to understand the effect of applying the proper principles in running your chosen field of business.

What happens in a supply chain is not as simple as what happens in other business-related structures since the management involves so many processes, ranging from the manufacturing phase up to the time when goods are then passed on to the expected recipient - the customer. Therefore, the supervision of a supply chain requires a steady and competent administration of the combined steps and application of an intellectual approach in the use marketing techniques and strategies in line with the set corporate goals.

In line with this intensive and exhaustive line of work, you as the manager, owner or CEO, have the task of overseeing the manufacture, distribution and the transport of the goods in the overall arrangement of things in a supply chain, and you must make sure that the demands of the business are met. Like for example, it is a primary requirement of the structure to have the availability of the right merchandise at the rightful area of process at every given time. Managing the supply chain almost translates to zero errors to keep everything in operation. Therefore, the companies and all other people that you involve should work in harmony and operate perfectly to achieve the expected output of a supply chain.

I am quite certain that you already have the perfect concept of what goes on in a supply chain. Now let us refresh ourselves with the persons behind the organization. It is important to identify the key players since this will bring us to understanding why the aspect of choosing the best possible supplier will lead to effective results to your business.

The mechanism behind the supply chain of a company is manned by several individuals. In a company that procures raw materials for manufacture, their key player is not only found behind the personas of the staff or employees of the company but particularly the ones providing stocks to a company in exchange for a given consideration. In short, you call them the suppliers. Developing a good relationship with your supplier is as important as acquiring the loyalty of clients and customers. This may not be evident, but this aspect of the business is often prone to mismanagement and neglect. There should be a strategic approach in maintaining a good rapport between the company and its key suppliers, since they are the ones who play a crucial role in ensuring the delivery of quality materials on time and contributing to the smooth phase of other relevant processes in the company. Since the end result is to provide the satisfying quality of either goods or services to the consumers of your products and services, you must be in the know of relevant indications of starting a good business relationship with a supplier. If you are starting your business anew, and still clueless about who can be a decent provider for your business needs then take what follows into consideration.

Almost every area of business requires that certain level and standard appropriate to the modern commercial industries are observed. Whether you are in the Construction, Medical, Automotive Industry, etc. there is a need in finding the right products and services to complete a job, redistribute, or personally consume. Knowing the appropriate factors to successful product procurement will enable you to overcome possible issues in the near future and run the business smoothly. It is key to partner with the right people who can add value, and most importantly add to the bottom line. In regards to the people overseeing the acquisition of products or services, it is imperative they have several qualities in which to look for.

Character

The first of these qualities is the Integrity of the buyer. The presence of integrity can help build trust between you and the persons with whom you transact with and allow efficiency in dealing with these people. Thus it is of the essence to be wise in choosing commitments that will involve the business and to harmonize conflicting issues to show that your company deals fairly and is a reliant business that they can trust. As a person with the power and authority to make financial decisions for your business, whether you're an Agent, Manager, or President of the company, there will be many individuals seeking to earn your business. Along with that, often times present "perks" of the job, in the form of gifts, dinners, outings etc. In and of itself there is nothing wrong with these types of relationship building activities. However, there may be times where these perks can cross a line and become a type of "bribe", likely benefiting the buyer at the expense of the company or business. Leaving opportunities for backdoor deals, overly inflated prices, and a poor reputation in the marketplace. When in doubt it is important to receive counsel from a manager, president, or another successful business person on acceptable extra-curricular activities. As the popular saying goes "hire for character and train for skill", be a person with character and integrity and always be learning.

Receptiveness to New Learning

In any role in society today it is absolutely essential to be "in the know" to stay at the top of your game. This is such an important attribute to building and maintaining an effective organization to efficiently prepare your business to face whatever lies ahead. There has never been another time in history where the availability of knowledge has been so successful. Which means you don't have to be rich or in a position of power to be able to exponentially grow in understanding, however that also means that if you don't make an effort to advance, you will very rapidly fall behind. There is an extensive range of information available to every person waiting to be accessed, about almost any topic and subject possible and it is not a surprise to know that business-related information is just one of them. There are many programs, books and blogs out there to help you in your journey, and when in doubt Google it! The technological world is very accessible and can provide you with relevant materials from which you can acquire additional information as well as brilliant ideas. It will be helpful for your goals to continually reinforce what you already know in relation to running the company in order to prepare you for future contingencies as your business grows. As you will find out when you begin to work at sharpening your skills, your income, expertise, and value will increase along with it.

A Good Purchaser Adds Value to the Company

Although an often overlooked topic, the ability to add value is among the top qualities of a procurement department. It is already an appreciated accomplishment for the company to observe the properly mandated protocols in doing a purchase for the organization, but employing reasonable strategies such as cost-saving initiatives can create a positive effect for the benefit of the business. The import of providing additional value to your company will result to cost minimization, thus added profit in the long run that counts as a contribution to the efficiency of the purchase department and corollary thereto, improving your worth as an asset of the business. Going beyond just buying at a good price, is invaluable to any organization. A great purchasing specialist has the ability to source innovative products, build relationships with suppliers and manage the "paper trail" in an organized manner. All of which can increase your internal costs, which we will touch on later.

The Proper Conviction of a Good Purchaser

The proper mindset is also key to achieving the objectives of your role in the company. It is part of your job description to perform tasks to achieve certain results that you are aiming for; which in the long run can produce valuable outcomes. It may help to go about the standard procedures as dictated by company policies in making the purchases relative to the needs of the company, but it will be a greater achievement to employ additional techniques to increase the benefits that the business can reap. Since the works of the mind are best measured through the actuations, the following reveals the proper means of employing the proper mindset to be an asset to the business. This brings you to incorporating key steps that may be helpful to achieve your specific business goals from the perspective of a purchaser.

The Good Purchaser knows that Researching is key! Keep in mind that the market is highly competitive and companies would love to make you their client. Thus competitors will offer the best prices that will suit your business. Plan to score the best deal for your company? Then it's a matter of canvassing for the best price available. This involves an aggressive approach to negotiating prices to get the best deals for the business.

The Good Purchaser is Always on the lookout for great deals! The strategic manner of purchasing entails doing the transaction just in time when discounts, sales promotions and rebates can be availed of will save your company a good amount of cash!

The Good Purchaser shares beneficial tips to make the smart inventory system and encourages his staff to participate. Involve your employees by making them responsible in keeping an up-to-date inventory with minimal issues. Contributors to the success will be rewarded. Sometimes, all it takes is to make a competition to encourage everyone's participation.

The Good Purchaser knows that Purchasing in Bulk equals savings for the company. Articles if purchased in large quantities improves the cost of acquisition compared to buying a unit at a time. It's then your initiative as the owner or purchasing agent to practice purchasing in bulk the items that the company needs. Just remember not to over-stock!

Chapter 6

Choosing the Right Supplier

"If a man will make a purchase of a chance he must abide by the consequences."
- Richard Richards

Just as with having the right people in place internally, it is equally important to have the right people outside the company to support your business. As a reiteration the relation with a supplier is as important as keeping the loyalty of your customers to the company or trade. A trusted partner who is able to accommodate and fulfill your buying needs is critical, as time is money and a good supplier can make the buying process a lot less stressful. Find someone who is of the utmost integrity, who you can trust, will work hard on your behalf, and suits your business needs.

Integrity Matters

Trust and integrity are important now more than ever in your business relationships. There are many people who will be making many empty promises to earn your business, but what's important is to truly build a relationship with a salesperson or company you can trust. You will agree that both trust and integrity are two things that are difficult to prove at once. Only the passage of time can tell and is the best possible test out there to conclude with finality if you can trust people whom you rely on to supply you with the items that you needed. If you are not yet aware of how trustworthy some individuals are should you plan to make deals with them in the future, then here are some questions that you should ponder about. These questions may not be enough to gauge everything, but it will provide you with a clearer perspective in dealing with chosen suppliers. Are your current suppliers willing to be straight with you, or do the right thing even at their own expense? Are they honest with you in their pricing and actions, or are you finding many inconsistencies?

Have you ever had a salesperson answer the phone with a "Hey, I was just getting ready to call you" or a "your delivery is on its way" just to find out that these assurances were frequently made and often misleading to your business' prejudice? Then you may have to start thinking twice about continuing with your business relations or allowing them to act as they please. As petty as it may seem these are signs of someone telling you what they think you want to hear, not what is actually at your best interest. Again these are they people who are assisting you in many of your day to day financial and business decisions. It is of the essence to evaluate the consequences of not receiving the appropriate support that a sound, running business will require. It may be of help to give them a little nudge by telling them straight issues that you want sorted out. Hey, a business is business, right?

Willing to Work for You

Too much to do and not enough time, that seems to be a universal trend these days. Are people really doing so much these days that it pits against their availability of occasions to perform these activities? Archimedes once said "Give me a lever long enough and a prop on which to place it, and I shall move the world". What a great quote on the principle of leverage! If you are in the predicament of managing the business with the limited amount of time to attend to some of the nitty-gritty details, then finding somebody who can do that for you will be such a great assistance. No need to look far and wide for this person! A great supplier/salesmen will offer you just that, the ability to do the legwork to multiply your availability to get more things done! Needing to research a part number; finding the right product for an application; or searching for a past invoice etc.? These are the things that a great support team will help you do! Surround yourself with a reliable group of people to help you get things done in your absence. Employ people who can work independently and are able to exercise discretion to work out details with minimal supervision. But of course rely on people whom you can trust! Inspire these people who work under you that the company's interest is a priority and for such they will be rewarded with what's due to them. Get creative with this though, since it was earlier mentioned that many people are vying for your business, but as you build a relationship, these people will go above and beyond with things like standing in your place for a meeting, or giving a training presentation to the rest of your team. In your absence they will keep your company in check.

Services

An important consideration when selecting your supply chain team is the quality of the services they provide. Keep in check these things related to supply chain management like delivery, installations, backorder replenishment, and the pertinent activities making this list go on. In a business where recurrent purchases occur, it is also very important to know the volume of the products you ordinarily utilize, the amount of stocks that you expect them to keep on hand and deliver to you when the need to restock arises, as well as the assortment of products that you can choose from should you decide to try some items with a different branding. It is relevant to the supply chain management to keep things organized and services provided when the need for them arrives. The main reason for this is that you want to be able to limit the number of suppliers you need to use, reduce backorders, and eliminate the paperwork on your end. The best starting point is to make a list of the most important goals for your business, from there you will best know how to interview and select the best supplier that fits your needs. These are one of the main areas to consider, even greater in significance to taking the prices into account.

Take Alternative Suppliers

Choosing your suppliers is essential to your business interest. But you cannot have to many supplying companies to buy from, as this is very difficult to manage and may be less on the cost-effective side. You may not want to surround yourself with too many suppliers, because nobody wants overstocking of the products, either. But in times of contingency, it is handy to have alternative suppliers that can provide you with materials you need to keep the business running. But as part of a good business strategy, it is not bad to keep substitutes. With them you may get the supplies you need in situations when a scheduled delivery, due to emergency and unforeseeable events, should arrive late. This way you will not worry about the continuity of your operations.
Other relevant pointers

Find suppliers who are willing to provide you with their quotations, and if they can manage, samples! If possible, meet the supplier face to face so you can effectively communicate and understand each other's' expectations in the start of the relationship. It is also the best time to look for someone who can give good terms and conditions with a willingness to negotiate. Also make sure that your supplier will actually do the work and not those people who outsource. If your supplier is one who does this in the conduct of your business, get to know the subcontractors. It is up to you to decide if you are fine with this arrangement to avoid issues in the future.

Chapter 7

Price is NOT the Only Criteria

"Price is what you pay, Value is what you get." – Warren Buffet

This may shock many people, however this is an important key point to remember. The usual conception when it comes to transacting in business is that "the price should be right" and price itself should be the primary consideration in dealing to get the advantage in one's business endeavors. But this mode of thinking could be erroneous because it insinuates that the best deals are often gauged in shedding minimal costs on the part of the procurer. This idea is actually reasonable but it is not the proper belief to succeed in running your chosen supply chain. The price should not be the sole consideration, since it is just one aspect of doing a purchase or any business transaction. There are several other factors at play, and the goal shouldn't be to get each and every item as cheap as possible. It is true that you pay for the quality that you may receive and to do business means you will not welcome poor quality or service. This necessitates changing how you should view the value of articles or services vis-à-vis the amounts that you are willing to spend for them. Always remember that good quality does not come cheap nor free. So a much better aspiration for any supply chain owner or manger is to reduce your overall "costs" that will in turn increase the bottom line profits without downgrading what we deem as the proper standard. We are going to look at a few of these factors; Quality, Added Value, and Relationships.

Quality

As Warren Buffet insinuated above, there is a correlation between price and Value. It would be valuable to look into the insight of the famed motivational speaker, who was also a very good salesman, Zig Ziglar, who has something of relevance to the discussion about quality which is far from what Buffet insinuates. Ziglar says it differently, that price may not be the same with value, when he asked his customer once "Are you referring to the price or cost? What is being said here is that there is a difference between the two, and it's important to be able to separate and calculate that difference in your mind? When talking about buying quality, we must understand that at times it may be spending more upfront to get a better "value" and return on the back end. For example, if you were to buy a saw blade for the cheapest price versus spending a little more, you would often find that the cheaper blade wouldn't get nearly as many uses out of it as you would the more expensive blade. Which means you may be buying 2 or even 3 times as many blades to get the same "Value" out of the higher priced blade. One Caveat with this goes back to the reminder, always be learning point, which is to know your products, and to use your relationship with your sales representative to properly look into the specifications of the items that you choose to ensure the benefits warrant the extra price. So better value after all warrants the extra price.

Added Value

You want your supplier(s) to have some intangibles that add value to your business by using their services. A few examples of these are as follows: having a salesman who can bring you innovative ideas is handy and advantageous-if he is someone who is recognizable in your industry. With his known reputation he can help refer leads to you, like recommending a company or business who is willing to package items together at a better cost for your business. Another one is securing the quality of the goods that you will acquire from this supplier. Keep in mind that a poor quality in the goods you produce will reflect negatively on your business and not to your supplier. The key here is being clear about what you want to achieve to benefit the business and being able to communicate to the supplier so both ends are met. The end result is that you can get the satisfactory results that you would like gain in accordance with your planned expectations. Again, refer back to your list of goals and requirements and look for qualities that can cut down on the matters that give you headaches as well as costing you money. If back orders are a problem, find someone who has systems in place to expedite the replenishment or who maintains a better in stock position than your current supplier.

Build Great Relationships

This cannot be said enough and is absolutely crucial in today's economy! Many business owners and purchasing people get this part wrong, often thinking that because they are the one writing the order they are in control and can take advantage of their superior position by making unreasonable demands, including personal "perks" as we touched on previously. Let's get this in the right perspective, we need good suppliers/distributors as a part of our team, and when you find them treat them like gold. Remember they are assets that once you lose, their sort will be difficult to come by. It will not only cost you headaches in finding good replacements to replenish your supplies but also limit your chances of striking better deals and product quality choices. It is very difficult to establish a great working relationship again and again with various suppliers and/or distributors so keep in mind to regularly deal and communicate with them not only professionally but also respectfully. Work hard at building and nurturing these relationships, and see the huge dividends it pays in your business. You will begin to see faster deliveries, more favorable lead times, faster quotes and responses back and the list goes on.

Begin to train yourself to look beyond making quick decisions based on price alone. Again, price can be a consideration but it is not the only important thing. People often gain in that which they have paid for. Use your list of goals/needs to keep you on track and seek the recommendations of your sales representative. With him/her it is highly probable that you have now built a solid relationship, based on trust with this person. Through a trusted sales representative, you can refer to his opinions to seize for those opportunities to help add value and increase profits for the benefit of your business.

Chapter 8

Become Efficient

"We are lost, but we are making good time." -Star Trek

Every human being can relate to the feeling, when you look back at your "busy" day, and wonder "what did I accomplish". There will always be inefficiencies in the things we do, but we can always improve on yesterday's inadequacies. The goal here is not to become perfect, but rather to train ourselves to recognize and become better in both our strengths and weakness'. Efficiency entails the achievement of predetermined goals and producing that desired outcome sans the wastage of efforts, capital, and energy among others. Indeed, as individuals we are not precluded from committing mistakes in the daily activities, however we can avoid errors to a minimum when it comes to business. In this realm, our useful output will be compared with the entire output as against the resources that we are able to utilize to assess the level of efficiency in making business decisions. What follows are some general pointers to incorporate and enhance efficiency in how to manage the needs of the supply chain and any other form of business.

Productivity is often related to what we consider as efficient in the work establishment since in the employment sector an efficient system in manufacturing or processing will have positive results in the production ratings of the firm. It is important to encourage productivity from your employees and the associated supply system. You can accomplish this by prescribing specific guidelines to govern your staff and monitoring the organization's progress in meeting the specific goals that were set relative to these guidelines. Although at present, there are many factors that hinder many workers or employees from being productive. Some of these factors include an imbalance when it comes to the amount of hours allotted for work to the actual time spent by the staff, misuse of company properties to unrelated tasks and other inappropriate activities such as unrestricted access to the web activities, among others which should have been times that must be allocated to render work. To address these issues that may plague the workplace in the long run and avoid jeopardizing the operations of your business, it is within your discretion in the management position to set things right. Keep to mind several points to understand the specific situation you are facing and set the workplace in the proper pace of the acceptable standard of day-to-day productivity.

Organize

The first area we can look at is our organizational skills. This will entail you to look into your specific habits and the manner of how you deal with the everyday basics related to your business and personal life. Perhaps it would be nice to do tis once in a while. Pause for a moment and take a look at your desk... need I say more? Like the saying goes "a cluttered desk equals a cluttered mind." To be efficient it is imperative to create the habit of being organized, this should be the foundation. With so many choices out there of productivity methods, from the standard filing cabinet to technology apps, it's important to keep things simple. Often the flood of choices creates confusion, which will lead to disorganization. Ponder the specific areas where you feel you can be more organized, and seek help from other who seem to have that area of their life under control.

In addition to what has been said, by starting to eliminate clutter you do not only delve on organizing your business, you can also be motivated to go straight to the work to finish the day's task.

Indeed, productivity is ensured by saving time. Going over piles of documents and cluttered stuff in search of a needed item will result to time wastage instead of using said opportunity to more valuable endeavors. Start by de cluttering your desks with items that are no longer working to acquiring equipment that performs several functions within a unit. There are more ways than you can think of to make time worthwhile in relation to your day's agenda.

It will also contribute to effective organization to generate storage space to place the clutter after tidying your workspace. Got no available space, you say? Then create one! The addition of shelves, storage boxes or units and cabinets will do the trick.

Sorting the mail will also add to your plan of organization. This will entail you to deal with mail that just recently arrived and throw away the mails that you consider as junk. Label emails and classify them according to how important they are. There are varied categories like bills, mails requiring urgent response, publications et cetera.

The maintenance of an efficient filing system will help you keep track of all documents that you may need in the future. You'll never know when these documents may come in handy for reference. Contracts with your chosen supplier, tax related receipts and other legal papers must be properly stored and easily accessible. With the advent of technology, you may include scanned copies of said documents other than the originals for easier reference whenever needed.

Keeping your computer organized is also key. Nowadays that most people turn to their personal computers to manage accounting and other related stuff using helpful soft wares, the arm yourself with the updated versions to ensure maximum efficiency in utilizing these applications. The necessity of doing a day-to- day inventory will be much easier using applicable software. Just make sure that like your desk space, your computer is likewise rid of unwanted files every now and then. Creating shortcuts of applications in your desktop will also facilitate easier access of relevant files. Last but not the least, get a good anti-virus program and for added security to your files, always create a back up.

Delegate

What enables top performers in any field or business to find success is the fact that they are surrounded by staff or people who are reliable and efficient. This contributes further to the betterment of the company by finding workers like these. As we touched on in chapter 2, the ability to leverage yourself, can transform how you work. In any business there are systems in place, some much better than others that provide you the ability to do just that. As a purchasing agent or owner you must recognize that you are really a "manager" of the buying process, rather than trying to be a master of all trades. Knowing your job by heart and working towards improving your skills to succeed in performing your roles will help you succeed in your company goals. This will not only involve your efforts but making sure that other company assets can be tapped to deal with existing predicaments that can be given practical solutions. Should you be unable to attend to an issue, you are in a position to know who among staff can effectively provide for a solution. For example, if you are having billing and invoicing issues, leverage your accountants' expertise or accounting department within your company to help solve, make phone calls on your behalf, etc. to quickly resolve these matters. Again, surrounding yourself with reliable people will help run your business with lesser problems, or should they arrive, issues are easily dealt with.

We understand the complexity that is often associated with managing several relationships in the supply chain. There must be an operational integration of various information, ideas, systems, processes and efforts to function properly and bring about a smooth flow of the procedures starting with the source-which is the supplier and other areas in the sequence. When you oversee the operation of the company, know the skills and capabilities of the people who work for you. Learn to delegate certain tasks to employees through official means such as a written authority. This will enable the staff that was given a delegated authority to sign contracts or enter into authorized purchases for and in behalf of the company. To avoid an issue arising from such delegation, limit the scope of authority handed to a trusted employee to a certain degree and delineate specific terms to clarify the situation. Make it a clear policy that everyone in the work place has the responsibility to be prudent by knowing what happens to the goods and services and to contribute to the well being of the company.

Tracking

Tracking inventory, monitoring given tasks, and evaluating how effective new decisions will turn out, will greatly impact your efficiency and effectiveness. In the aspect of doing an inventory, the awareness of what product is coming in and which items will be going out will obviously help assist you in producing effective decisions in the future when it comes to buying needs and keeping tabs on your supplies. The ability to keep track of the resources in the company through a well-organized inventory will help you save on money and costs. There's a funny joke as follows "The easiest way to find that missing inventory is to place a new PO!" This is not good advice but I'm sure you can relate with the humor in this statement. It also pays to set a schedule and sticking to the same. It is very important in keeping track of your daily, weekly tasks, which could easily be included in the organization category as well. Lastly, anytime a new decision or process is implemented, it is vital to keep record of the results of that decision, to ensure that it is increasing your productivity, profit, and reputation. Otherwise you may just be adding another step into your already busy routine.

Chapter 9

Taking Action

"DO IT NOW!!!"

Now that we have gone over the basics of what the role of a purchasing agent/person is, what to look for in a reliable supplier, how to be efficient in handling purchases, etc., it is now time to put these theories into action. It has been said by Thomas Jefferson, a former President, and one of the founders of the United States of America in one of his notable quotes," Do you want to know who you are? Don't ask. Act! Action will delineate and define you." Doing real business may involve taking risks and jumping into the unknown but these unknown leaps may be the key to finding success in the field. Just remember not every business was off to a good start when they began, particularly in the initial stages of their operation. The attainment of success in the business industry, particularly on the part of the purchasing agent necessitated changing direction when things did not turn out the way they expected, and rely in their experience coupled with a prudent business judgment to lead the company to greater heights. Thus it is of the essence to take the first step, doing it forward one step at a time, take time to learn valuable lessons and aim for growth. There are a lot of information available that can expand your theoretical knowledge and perspective, but taking the initiative by putting these theories to test is the groundbreaking step.

Steps that you can take:

Find something that you can learn that will add value to your
company or business and improve your character. And you will be
surprised that you can never ran out of good ideas. First note, you
know, you may be developing a very good strategy or technique in
your head right at this moment but there are just too many
negative ideas that pop alongside this brilliant concept. Still
confused if your idea is feasible? Then I say if you have thought
about this technique long enough, and saw that the advantages
outweigh the negatives, and then put your theory to the test. Start
by starting in a small scale accompanied with a limited risk then
increase your stake along the way if your strategy should prove to
be effective later on. On the second note, bolster that resolve in
yourself that your character and approach will build your business.
Giving things up at the first instance of failure was never an
effective attitude when you commit yourself to accomplishing your
business goals. Undoubtedly, many agree that persistence in the
use of business techniques is key!

Make a list of the important factors that the right supplier would
provide. Before you can accomplish this, it is imperative for you to
know about your needs as a prospective recipient of provisions
from your chosen supplier. It takes more than going through the
copies of price lists presented to you while you are making your
choice, nor is it about relying on your intuition as a buyer. This is a
crucial part of your business, so you should know that there is very
little room for mistakes in this aspect, since the failure to deliver
on the part of your chosen supplier will have a drastic effect in the
operation of your business. The following are the keys, DECIDE
WHAT YOU NEED, IDENTIFY PROSPECTIVE SUPPLIERS
THAT ARE RELIABLE and finally PICK THE SUPLIER OF YOUR
CHOICE. A simple manner of presenting these points is to
pinpoint the qualities of an effective supplier. Go back to the
earlier discussion in the earlier chapter about choosing the right
supplier. You will nonetheless conclude that the good sort will
offer you selection of products and/or services that can keep up-or
even go beyond your expectations as to what they can provide.

Lastly, it is wiser to determine at the onset the necessary number of suppliers that you think your company might need after considering possible contingencies. Carefully choosing a group of suppliers from your selected lot will make it easier for you to control your stocks and give you the extra benefit of gaining something more by getting the good deals that only familiar suppliers are willing to provide.

Take your time interviewing your sales representative to ensure he is a person of character; he can provide innovative ideas, and in possession of the willingness to work on your behalf. Where is this going? This is about you recognizing a reliable contributor to your business affairs. Since you are dealing for a supply chain in the background, then the conduct of business is partly founded on the expectation that you are dealing with somebody that you can trust. In return they can also have the confidence that you will also do your part of the deal. Also be flexible. Your position will gain you unsolicited advice but this may be more helpful than you might think. You may already have clear images of the products that you wanted to acquire relevant to the business but it will not hurt to be receptive to reasonable information. Ask these questions to your sales representative and if he gives the response that will suit your business needs, then he is the one that you can rely upon.

- Can he accelerate the speed of delivery during times of distribution?
- Are they efficient and accurate in bringing to you the volume of products that you would require at a given time?
- Can they supply good quality products and services at reasonable costs?

Search for some areas where you can find value in buying a more expensive product, but would save you money in the long run. Managing a supply chain business can tempt you in procuring the best products at the lowest possible rates to save on cost. But always keep in mind that quality should never be compromised. The lowest price is not all the time the best value for your money. If you expect superior quality and reliability from those articles that your supplier provides it may demand from you to reevaluate the price that you are prepared to pay in exchange for these deliveries. Note, there are several matters that you would wish to balance in this purchasing process: service and product quality, the budget and the consistency or availability of your supplies.

Select two people in which you can develop a stronger relationship with, one internal one external. When dealing with people outside the company, it would be best to use a partnership approach. This way a strong relationship between your company and your trusted supplier will be secured. Let the suppliers recognize that your business is as important as to them as their other clients and you demand of them the best service that they can provide. Reciprocate this by letting them feel that they are also important to your business and its unhampered operation as a chain. Within the company, you should delegate the responsibilities to a staff that you know is trustworthy and reliable, and can manage the given tasks with minimal supervision.

Determine the areas that you are good at. It is like determining your personal strengths and weaknesses but this time focus on the aspects that will make you more able in handling your company responsibilities. Success in managing any business is not about possessing all the desirable traits of a good manager. The most successful CEOs, businessmen and managers were after all individuals with their own set of flaws. Nor were they perfect in all of their business decisions. They were able to succeed since they were able to exceed their capacity as decision makers in their respective companies. It is more about knowing your skills and capabilities, and sharpening these skills that you can apply to make good business judgments.

This book may have provided you with good insights that you can utilize, but still it is of great importance that those points that you have read and referred back to throughout this book are reduced to real business applications. Whenever you take the initiative to transform ideas into actions, no matter how small and insignificant, it will create a lasting impression to your brain. Slowly but surely, this routine will encourage you to continue doing things in the same way thus fostering good habits in the long run. Never allow delay to take a toll on your level of productivity. You need to come to the realization that these small steps that you take towards achieving what you want will later have their own weight in gold. "Mastery over procrastination, DO IT NOW!"

Chapter 10

The Goals and Purpose of Supply Chain Management

The very definition of supply chain management indicates that it is not a simple job; it is a complex task that extends way beyond the scope of a single company and a great deal of effort is required to build up a reliable supply chain network and maintain it. This means there is the need for a substantial action list, a list that takes time, money and expertise. Strategies are needed, relationships have to be built, roles defined, processes aligned and the people involved have to be developed sufficiently to handle what is expected of them.

Given all of this, you might wonder if supply chain management is actually worthwhile and to that, I would have to say yes. Any organization, no matter what the industry is, needs a strong supply chain to compete in a tough marketplace. And that supply chain is needed if you are to stay n budget throughout your entire project and deliver when you say you will. The following are the top five goals and purposes of good supply chain management.

Achieve Fulfillment Efficiently

This is the most basic goal of supply chain management – to make sure you have the inventory ready to meet customer demand. There is an old adage that fits this goal very nicely – "you can't sell from an empty wagon". Even in construction this works – you have to be able to fulfill your clients requirements efficiently, on time and with no hitches.

All organizations have to ensure that they build supply and demand into their supply chain model and they do this by employing cross-chain resources in the most efficient way possible. All partners in the supply chain must be able to work together to ensure maximum productivity, come up with a set of standard processes, cut out duplications and keep inventory to a minimum. All of this ensures that there is no waste, costs are driven down and the supply chain is efficient.

The most important part of this goal is to reduce supply chain expenses, especially in times of global economic upheaval, when capital conservation is the most important. Building in efficiency initiatives allow the organization to focus on any specific aspect of the supply chain to cut costs where possible – the two most popular targets for cost cutting are inventory and transportation. Between them, these two can account for around 81% of logistic systems costs in US businesses – about $1.08 trillion.

An agricultural co-operative called Ocean Spray managed to reduce their freight costs by opening up a new distribution center in Florida. Because of this, the distance to some locations was reduced significantly and was in the perfect position to take advantage of empty railroad boxcars that were on route from New Jersey to Florida. Moving from trucks on the road to using the rails, together with a significant cut in outbound mileage, meant that they could reduce their freight costs by around 40% and their carbon dioxide emissions by 20%.

Another case study is Kimberley Clark, personal care product manufacturers. For 6 years, they have been working hard to come up with a supply chain that is demand driven and, by realigning their network of distribution centers and streamlining their facilities, they have managed to remove inventory and related costs from their system.
In a further move, they switched to demand planning software

using retailer POS (point of sale) data to better understand and come up with new forecasts. The result of this is that they have reduced their inventory of finished stock by 19%, which represents substantial savings in the supply chain.

Customer Value Must be Driven

While it is important to focus on efficient fulfilment and keeping costs down, a supply chain management system also has to look at creating value for all of their customers. These customers are the heart of the business because, without them, there wouldn't be a business and there would be no need to create the supply chain. As such, this is one of the most basic goals in any supply chain management program – to meet the needs of the customer consistently and, where possible, exceed their requirements.

All of this begins with a customer service strategy, market-driven, based entirely customer requirements – at this point, it is vital that these requirements are understood by every person in the chain. Every other objective, strategy or goal in the supply chain has to come from the basic requirement to provide value to the customer. Done properly, the result will be a higher quality of service and less problems to deal with.

Just-in-time (JiT) delivery is critical to me industries, including the food service and restaurants. McCain Foods are the biggest manufacturer of French fries in the world and, instead of opting for rail delivery, which would be cheaper; instead, they chose to work together with a long-haul truck carrier. This ensures that their deliveries are made on time to all of their time-sensitive businesses that rely on them. The trailers are preloaded, they secure extra capacity and the deliveries are expedited as and when required to make sure that those French fries are always on the menu.

Goals 1 and 2 must not be mutually elusive. For true success, every organization must balance efficiency and effectiveness in their supply chain to ensure that they deliver optimal performance.

Organizational Response Enhancement

Another of the most basic goals of supply change management is the response to change. In the current climate, rapid change is inevitable and businesses must deal with multiple forces that will change the way they work and determine their survivability. Good supply chain management will help the organization to adapt to all of these changes, including economic upheaval, globalization, changing customer needs and any other issues related to these.

Global trade has seen unprecedented expansion in recent years and this serves to make the competition fierce from new entrants to the market. Whereas once the likes of Phillips, Sony, Panasonic and Samsung would have had their own shelf space in the stores for televisions, now they must share it with any number of dozens of new entrants.

Right now, global trading costs are on the rise; offshore labor has gone up and, as such, no longer can global trading guarantee you can offer the lowest price. This is where supply chain management steps in with their flexibility and expertise in analyzing and providing the right response to these issues. Conversely, globalization does provide huge opportunities for expansion and those with flexible and professional supply chain management in place are in the best position to take advantage of that.

The current economic crisis, and those that have gone before, have an exceptionally high impact on the demand from customers and on production levels. The organizations that are not ready, the ones who do not anticipate what will happen and adjust their capacity accordingly are the ones who will not survive – and it isn't necessarily the smaller businesses that fall, either. The last few years have some big names crashing out of the game and much of it comes down to ineffective supply chain management.

Economic downturns tend to run on a cycle and, although they can happen sooner than expected, there are always market signs. Recessions do not happen overnight and the survivors of the fallout will always be those who build a model into their supply chain for dealing with the changes that these crises bring. The supply chain has to be flexible and it has to have a structure of variable costs. Standardized systems and processes, built in at the start, will also help an organization to cope with short notice changes to demand and will keep the financial chain on target.

Today, the word has the internet; it has information at its beck and call and, because of that, consumers can make the strongest of demands on any supply chain. The consumer no longer has to accept what one company offers when they can check out 100 others; they can check up on product reviews, compare price between companies and check the stock availability right from their computer or smartphone. This raises expectations; they want more variety, they want goods that are customized, they want to be able to buy off-season and they want it quickly and cheaply. As a result, retailers have to be able to make use of Omni channel capabilities – inventory must be a shared resource and they need to make use of something called "distributed order technology" to be able to fill these orders on time.

Add to all of this the shorter life cycle of products, new technologies coming out to change supply chains and raised government regulations of the processes in the supply chains and you have a very good reason to ensure that your supply chain management is on the ball and is flexible.

Build Up Resiliency in the Network

Over the course of time, any organization can expect business challenges to arise and they should have plans in place to deal with those. However, they also need to be able to deal with sudden disruptions to the supply chain, disruptions that may, on occasion, be severe. These are not your everyday, typical event; they could be caused by severe weather disruption, natural disasters, failure of suppliers, labor strikes, etc. No matter what causes it, these events cause a significant negative effect on the supply chain and can make the organization vulnerable to damages to reputation, finances and other relational damage. One research study as shown that glitches in the supply chain can be associated to a decrease in shareholder value that is beyond normal expectations.

Given how much disruptions of this nature can cost a business it is vital that the supply chain management builds in plans for dealing with such scenarios. Steps include risk assessment, risk identification, and risk reduction. In order to cut the risk of vulnerability to disruptions of this nature, it is recommended that organizations build in redundancy to the supply chain, collaborate on safety and security and cross train people as a form of investment.

As well as taking preventative measures in terms of risk management, it is also vital for organizations to build in disruption management techniques. They must include the capability to be able to spot a disruption, overcome it and make changes to stop it happening again in the future. For risks that are already identified, the supply chain must be designed in such a way that it can come back quickly from a major disruption. For risks that are identified as potential, not very likely to occur risks, but ones that would cause catastrophic effects, contingency plans must be built in to the supply chain and they must be thoroughly tested.

A case study on Dell Inc., a company that is known for providing CTO (configure to order) computer systems, shows that their supply chain has been configured to cut risk and to bounce back quickly from any major disruption. Their configure to order process allows the company to deal with shortages of components by configuring systems in alternative ways and by trying to get customers to order systems made with components that are readily available.

Dell has also built up very strong relationships with their primary suppliers so that their customers are given priority when supplies face uncertainty. Lastly, the organization constantly reviews their secondary suppliers to cut down on the risk of shortages of inventory. It was strategies like these that averted a major crisis for the company after the 2011 earthquake in Tohoku, Japan.

Ensure Financial Success

Perhaps the most important role of any supply chain management is to ensure financial success for the company. Typical initiatives are focused on cost efficiency – streamlining levels of stock to cut down on the cost of carrying inventory, automating fulfillment operations to cut down on labor costs, consolidating orders to reduce transportation costs, etc. In direct contrast to this, many of the top businesses use their supply chain to increase their sales and get into new markets as quickly as possible. Their main goal is to push a competitive advantage and their value for the shareholders.

One thing that helps executives recognize the true value of supply chain management is a dual focus on generating revenue and cutting costs. More and more emphasis is placed on supply chain management these days and it is important that executives can manage the complexities that are both cross-functional and cross-company.

Chapter 11

The Key to Success in Supply Chain Management

When it comes to supply chain management, automating it is one of the most difficult of all the software projects you will ever undertake. Consider these case studies:

NCR, based in Dayton, Ohio, spent more than $7 million on software applications for their supply chain, none of which produced any return to start with. The reason for that was because many of the most important employees in the chain would not use them.

Plasti-line, a sign-maker company based in Knoxville, Tennessee, completed their supply chain project only to find that the ERP system they put in place did not work with the supply chain software applications they were using.

What it boils down to is this – very few companies have been able to automate their supply chains successfully. So, why should you bother? Simply because, it is well worth the time, the effort and the money to implement the right supply chain software and get it right. Take NCR for example; when they eventually got their system running properly – and got their staff to use it –, it saved the company millions of dollars by moving the ownership of their inventory away from their warehouses to the suppliers.

Because of better planning, Plasti-Line has managed to cut their manufacturing head count down by a significant 34%. For both companies, the savings are welcomed in the current tough economic crisis, when many companies struggle to remain efficient and effective. So, to help you automate your construction supply chain, here are five ways to make the savings:

Sell to the Suppliers

This is the hardest part. Supply chain automation is exceedingly difficult. This is because it is so complex, it is outside the scope of your organization. Your employees have to change how they work as doe each person from each supplier that you add in to your supply chain.

The only people that can actually force these extreme changes down the throats of their suppliers are the largest and the most powerful of manufacturing companies. The rest of us have to try to sell the system to our suppliers, something that I would bet not many CIOs have ever had to do. This means a complete change, not just in the way you work but in the way you think too. Add to that the fact that these systems could be seen as a threat to your suppliers and you can see why it is so tough.

Let's go back to NCR. When they wanted to move ownership of at least some of their inventory to the suppliers, they had a tough job to convince those suppliers that they would benefit from this. In order to convince them, their director of supply chain management had to meet, face to face, with the executives of their largest suppliers and push home just how the new system would be of benefit to everyone involved.

Clearly, at every meeting he attended, he had one message – take on our systems and we will increase our business with you. Not only that, we will push other manufacturers your way as well. They faced a great deal of resistance to begin with but now around 40% of NCRs inventory is held at the suppliers, not in their own warehouses.

Stop Employees from Relying on Phones and Faxes

If you think it is tough to sell supply chain software to your suppliers, wait until you start trying to sell it to your staff. Your operations people are used to dealing with people and problems via the phone, a fax, or notes scribbled down on pieces of paper and there is a very high chance they will want to stay working that way. It is down to you to convince them that using automation is the way forward, that it will be well worth the time and money because, if you can't convince them they will find a way to work around it.

EP blots out old ways by removing the old legacy systems in place, while supply chain software isn't quite so harsh – just because you implement the software, it doesn't mean that you can take out the faxes and the phones they are still needed.

A good example of how not to do it comes from Keihin Aircon North America, a company who got their internal sales pitch totally wrong. The biggest stumbling block for the company was that they took things too far in trying to keep staff happy when it became one of the first companies to use supply chain software from Glovia. The vice president of operation admits that, when the system was installed at one of their plants in Indiana, they over-customized the interfaces, in specific the order-entry interfaces that were used for sending the orders out to suppliers. The reason they did it was to keep one group of employees who didn't like the standard interfaces happy.

He says that staff found it hard to give up the way they were working and the spreadsheets they used in order to adopt something more centralized. To make one small group of employees happy, a group that showed distinct unwillingness to adopt change, the VP went ahead and customized more than 30% of the system so that it matched up with the way they currently worked. The company spent a great deal of money in doing that - $100,000 which, in 1996, when the hangover happened, was a great deal of cash. That bill was five times more than their original plan.

It doesn't end there though; in fact, it gets worse. Because Keihin Aircon customized the software, when things went wrong they struggled to get the help they needed from Glovia. In the same way as many vendors, the company do not provide support to customizations of their software and by doing that, Keihin actually removed the responsibility for the software from the supplier to himself or herself. To get round that, Keihin had to employ a further three employees, all full time, at a salary of $50,000 a year each, to help with the system and, to this day, those employees are still in place, supporting the changes made all those years ago.

When you customize a system like this, it makes things so mu carder when you want to upgrade it. When Glovia issued updates to their supply chain software, Keihin struggled to implement them. All of the parts that had been customized had to be rewritten so that they fit into the new updated version.

Keihin learned from that and, when the system was implemented in another plant, they didn't go with the customized scheme. The employees at this plant had already heard of the major problems that occurred at the first plant and they understood that they had to learn the new system. While it was difficult, learning the new system was a one-off – it wouldn't have to be done again, whereas rewriting software that has been customized is a job for life.

Keihin eventually got together with Glovia to come up with a system that was in line with the need of the employees and with the support that Glovia could provide. That investment has paid off for Keihin but a very harsh lesson was learned by all. Sacrificing the integrity of a system to keep a handful of employees happy is simply not worth it, in terms of the money it cost, the time and the fallout. That mistake cost Keihin – they had a

$980,000 budget and it cost them 20% more - $1.2 million.

Going back to NCR, the employees that were the most against change were the ones who had to learn, not just the system but a new way of working overall. For example, on single customer service component of the new system moved the emphasis away from the simple and well tested method of a telephone call to a process of decision making that put most of the responsibility into the hands of the customer service operator – along with that, they were made to be more accountable too. Not everyone was happy with that, perhaps understandably, and it didn't take long for them to find ways around the new system.

To help things along, NCR brought in outside consultant to help train up the staff to use the new system. They also started an incentive program that put internal project management in line for promotion, and a whole host of other benefits for successfully getting staff to take up the new system.

Efforts were almost entirely focused on the 20% of staff who steadfastly refused to use the new system. It was explained to these people how the system worked and how, if they refused to adopt it, the whole system would fall apart. They were told that the company would not be able to maintain its integrity with supplier and would not be able to recognize any return on investment. That would result in the company going down the tubes. On the other side, these consultants and manages did listen to these employees and allowed them to have their say on what was frustrating about the system. Once the employees understood all of this, they accepted the new system and the supply chain could function smoothly once again.

Be Prepared for Bad Information

Unfortunately, there is a nasty twist to getting your employees to accept a news supply chain software system. New systems process the data exactly as they are programmed to do. However, this kind of technology cannot take the history of the company into account and it cannot absorb the processes that happen in the months that follow the system being implemented. The supply chain management has to understand and accept that, to begin with, the information that comes out of the system will need a little tweaking to get it right. If they are not forewarned, they will very quickly come to the conclusion that the system simply doesn't work.

In one example, a major automotive industry supplier put in new software for supply chain forecasting to try to predict the levels of demand for a particular product. Just before they did this, an automaker submitted an order for an oversized number of units. The system predicted that demand for this unit would be huge, based on just one single order.

If the company had followed the number spewed out by the system, it would have led to large numbers of orders for the materials for the product being issued to suppliers down the chain. Luckily, the problem was caught before it got to that but only when a forecaster ignored the numbers from the system and used his own.

However, that led to another problem – the forecasters lost their fate in the system and would only word using their own data. Like Keihin and NCR, this company had to customize the system and then start the long task of rebuilding their employees' confidence in the system. Once they understood that their expertise would be merged with the increasing accuracy of the new system, they accepted it and started to use it.

Fix the Connection Between ERP and Supply Chain

No doubt, you have already heard that, once you complete your ERP project the next natural step is to install the new supply chain software. The two systems do work well together – ERP captures the information for data, products, finances and inventory and gives it to the supply chain software so that it can predict the demand and keep the material supplies flowing smoothly through the entre chain.

Unfortunately, although it sounds all well and good, that relationship does not mean integration is easy. It is almost a given that the supply chain software you choose is not going to interface with your ERP system cleanly.

Supply chain software needs to be provided with a detailed map telling it how the products are put together on the assembly line, otherwise, in effect, it is worthless. Plasti-Line's new software for production scheduling had to take into account a large number of steps that were needed to produce a sign o that it could schedule the work efficiently. The trouble is, the ERP system used by Plasti-Line, the system that held the information the other system needed, didn't work that way.

The ERP system would document the entre process in separate linear steps. The supply chain system, on the other hand, the system designed to execute the entire process, handled the whole process as a bunch of steps that all get done together. In order to get both systems on the same wavelength, Plasti-Line had to rework their ERP system so that it matched with the way the supply chain system worked. A full time engineer was assigned to this job and the IS team had to carry out some reprogramming so that the bills of material were redefined and rerouted in the system based on the physical process of making the sign. After the system was whipped into shape, the number of people employed to make the signs was cut from 69 down to 45, representing a substantial savings.

Eliminate Conflict

Supply chain software is responsible for putting CIOs into conflict with the people who are responsible for managing the supply chain on a daily basis. These people do have a large chip on their shoulders mainly because they have been dog the job for years, without the need for a piece of software. Not only that, logistics and procurement have long been seen as second-class jobs, mundane and boring in almost every industry except for retail.

The people that do these jobs are not used to having others snooping in on what they do and the CIOs have to learn how to deal with those who are likely to shut the door firmly in their faces. NCR decided that they wanted to work out what the requirements were for the business without IT telling them what they could and could not do. Therefore, at the start of the planning process, IT were deliberately left out of the loop. Thus, NCR were able to come up with a hypothetical system, which was then put to IT to help with the technology and related matters. Because they didn't have any chance to help with improving the focus of the project, IT became nothing more than tactical installers. This, in their eyes, reduced their value and their input.

It is important to remember that, without the IT department, things can go horribly wrong so it is important for CIOs to become advice givers and facilitators, instead of being critics. When the current vice president of IS at Aviall Services, based in Dallas, first took office, the company were in the middle of upgrading their supply chain system. He made it clear that it was up to the IS team to help the users learn the new system. The first thing he had to deal with was an "our side or theirs?" attitude but the team did come round and the supply chain system at Aviall is now a complete success.

Automating the supply chain is something that can change the face of a business – for better or worse is all down to implementation and training. The risks are enormous but the potential for reward is much bigger. The companies that got it right and even the ones that got it completely wrong all know that every single link in the chain has to be strong. That takes incredible effort from every person in the business – one weak link and the whole lot will crumble, and that can spell financial disaster for any industry.

Provided they combine the deep desire to serve the needs of the business with a strong dose of reality, it is possible for CIOs to lead the supply chain. They must take on the task of picking the vendors very carefully, to manage implementations of technology and come up with as many solutions as needed for the desires of the business leaders in terms of system implementation.

The final step is to sell it. If your business and every person in the supply chain does not fully embrace the new system, it will all be a complete waste of time and money, not to mention effort. The way forward for any company, no matter how large or small they are, is supply chain software. Get it right and the rewards will be significant.

Chapter 12

6 Vital Supply Chain Metrics

Are your current supply chain metrics not helping as much as they possibly should be? Sometimes they don't and that is bad news because the metrics are the very basis of the S&OP process (Sale & Operations Planning). The supply of the supply chain metrics s actually in an endless supply so which ones should you be using to make your supply chain work as it should? These are six most important metrics that you should be employing.

Budget vs Demand and Forecast

This is an easy one. Every single month you should compare your yearly budget sales volume with the actual demand and the forecast that remains of the calendar year. What this does is lets you see if you are above or below your budget.
If the forecast and the sales come in over budget, you know that you can get through a period of speeding up operations but, if they are under budget, you will need to slow things down.

While this is one of the easiest of all the metrics to track, it is also the single most valuable one.

Forecast Error

The metric for your forecast error is based on your business but it has to tell you exactly how good or how bad you are at forecasting. Forecasting is one of the hardest things to do but supply chain planning isn't – or it shouldn't be. You shouldn't be striving for perfection; instead, you should be on the lookout for reasons, patterns that tell you why your forecast isn't right.

One of the best ways to do this is to use a men absolute percent method, based on the historic performance of the business over the last 6 months. This helps to keep things a little smoother and should stop you from going out of control when a one-off issue has an adverse effect on performance. Focus on the high-level trends and insights, not the one-off's.

Forecasting that is over optimistic or pessimistic can cause a problem so, if this s the case, you should use the forecast bias metric. Alternatively, if you are looking for a lot more detailed information, you could use a metric that calculates the SKU percentage that is performing above a specified forecast error. You could also weight those SKUs by revenue or volume so you only get the stuff that has the greater impact.

Forecast Change

This is also known as forecast evolution and it involves comparing the last forecast with the current one and see what the changes are, if any. Choose a set time period and combine volume into one unit of measure for both of the forecasts.

For example, let's assume that you are looking at the forecast for 202, the whole year. Go back to November 2011 and look at what you said the forecast would be; compare that against October 201. If you see huge changes from one month to the next, you have a big problem.

As a supply chain manager, you can only be as good as your forecast. Provided the data you start with is consistent, the easier you will find it to plan

Customer Service

Every organization should have some kind of metric for customer service and if you don't have one, you need to start asking why. Your supply chain is designed around your ability to get orders delivered to your customers, no matter what industry line you work in.

As with all metrics, this one is dependent on your business but it will usually be some type of line fill rate metric. The targets will vary from industry to industry - for some industries, less than 100% customer service can be a complete disaster while for others, the cost of providing 100% customer service may have a detrimental effect on operations.

Inventory Turns

First off, this metric has to represent the inventory turns for the entire supply chain, not just the finished goods at the distribution center. If you are only measuring those, you are not getting a proper insight into the inventory that could be building up further along the supply chain.

Let's assume that you are turning your inventory for the total supply chain twice every year. You have a production lead of four months and you keep two months' worth of buffer inventory in stock. This indicates that things are going well.

We could say that both inventory turns and customer service is trending upwards and, if that were the case, then your business is doing well.

David Pollock

Inventory Write-Off

It is a real shame, but inventory write-off happens in every business. In effect, you are wiping out some of the cash off your balance sheet, just tossing it in the bin. When you manage a supply chain, you have to treat the money from the business as if it were your own cash. If you are finding that the level of write-off is high, you have to look at why and then you have to implement some kind of plan to stop it from happening.

Maybe the sizes of your batches are not matching up with demand or with expected shelf life or maybe your quality issues are resulting in entire batches being rejected. Whatever the reason, inventory write-offs have to be looked into and, where possible, they have to be avoided.

Those are the top six metrics that you should be using to measure the performance and effectiveness of your supply chain. There are plenty others that you can use, just make sure that you get the right insights on performance and that you can clearly see how the business is performing in terms of every objective – including and most importantly, finances.

Conclusion

We went through some principles that you can incorporate to effectively run a supply chain in the view that these will lead to better results to your company. But just as you have found all the right reasons why you must be able to find a good supplier for your business, then here are further motivating factors that should encourage you why you should maintain a lasting relationship with a chosen supplier to keep the company running.

Accordingly, there is an innovative approach to managing the relationship between your business and your key suppliers that are proven to be beneficial to both parties. This strategy employs means and methods that enable a two-way channel for both the company and the supplier to effectively communicate and provide fair explanations to matters that seek resolution, particularly those of great relevance to the business transaction. Since they play a major role in your business, the suppliers that you choose must turn out to be reliable and can meet the demands of your business. Through the so-called Strategic Relationship Management, the relationship between you and your suppliers will be properly developed after. The insights shared in this book can revolutionize your methods of achieving goals in the supply chain management, starting with finding a good supplier for the best interest of your business.

Overall, the management of a supply chain is never easy with all the intensive processes that it involves. Likewise, it is a helpful note that applying wise market strategies can help the administration of the company a bit more convenient and less demanding. But as the time progresses, the companies are also faced with various matters that they must address, such as but not limited to the surge in the number of other companies ready to compete, the complexity of modern life, economic inflation and pertinent governmental measures imposed to regulate the conduct of trade and other industries that may directly or indirectly influence many corporate structures. But at the end of the day, still it your job to lead the business to achieving one of the primary objectives of managing a supply chain-that is to optimize the flow of the players within a supply chain. Furthermore, the end goal is to ensure that the customers are provided the opportunity and they can get their hands on the products or service that they need at the right time and place.

www.ingramcontent.com/pod-product-compliance
Lightning Source LLC
Chambersburg PA
CBHW060409190526
45169CB00002B/819